Investigating Science

What does a magnet do?

Jacqui Bailey

W
FRANKLIN WATTS
LONDON • SYDNEY

This edition 2010

First published in 2005 by Franklin Watts
338 Euston Road
London NW1 3BH

Franklin Watts Australia
Level 17/207 Kent Street
Sydney, NSW 2000

A CIP catalogue record for this book
is available from the British Library.

Dewey number: 538

ISBN: 978 0 7496 9616 0

Printed in Malaysia

Franklin Watts is a division of Hachette Children's Books, an
Hachette UK company.

www.hachette.co.uk

Series editor: Rachel Cooke
Editor: Jennifer Schofield
Design: Rachel Hamdi/Holly Mann
Picture researcher: Diana Morris
Photography: Andy Crawford, unless otherwise acknowledged

Acknowledgements:
Gerard Dryer/Africa Imagery/Afripics/Photographers Direct: 18t.
Vanya Edwards/Sovfoto/Eastfoto/Photographers Direct: 29b.
Simon Fraser/SPL: 20t. Ray Moller: 3.NASA: 28. Eric Needham/
Ecoscene: 22. Tony Page/Ecoscene: 29c. Sinclair Stammers/SPL: 7b.
Watts: 27b.

With thanks to our models: Chandler Durbridge, Charlie Spicer,
Ashleigh Munns, Emel Augustine, Keyon Duffus

Every attempt has been made to clear copyright.
Should there be any inadvertent omission please
apply to the publisher for rectification.

Contents

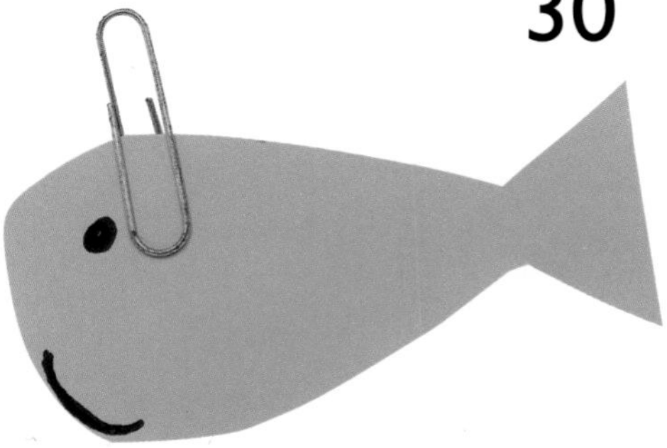

What are magnets?

Magnets are pieces of metal or stone that can make things stick to them.

THINK about the kinds of magnet you may have seen.

- Some toys have magnets in them.
- Magnets come in all shapes and sizes.

Have you ever played with a magnet?

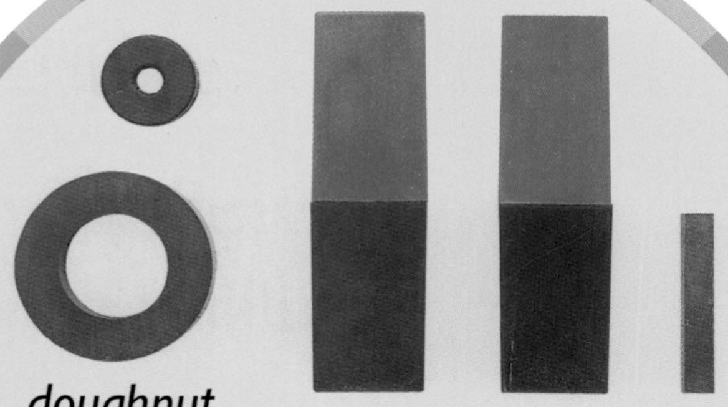

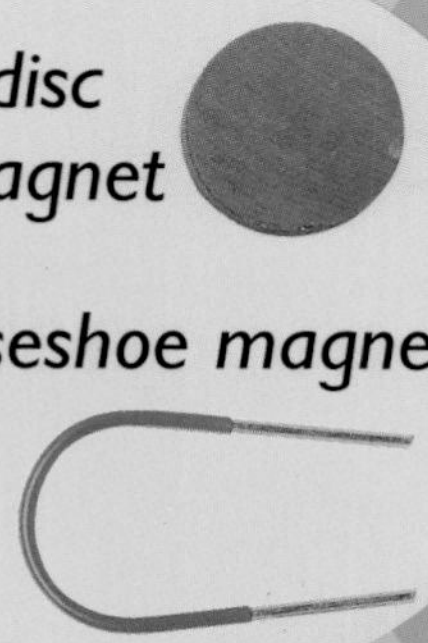

You will need:

- Scissors ✔
- Some string ✔
- A long pencil or a piece of dowelling ✔
- A doughnut magnet ✔
- Some coloured card ✔
- A permanent marker ✔
- Some metal paperclips ✔

What do magnets do?

1. Cut a length of string longer than your pencil or dowelling. Tie one end to the pencil and the other end to the magnet. This is your 'fishing rod'.

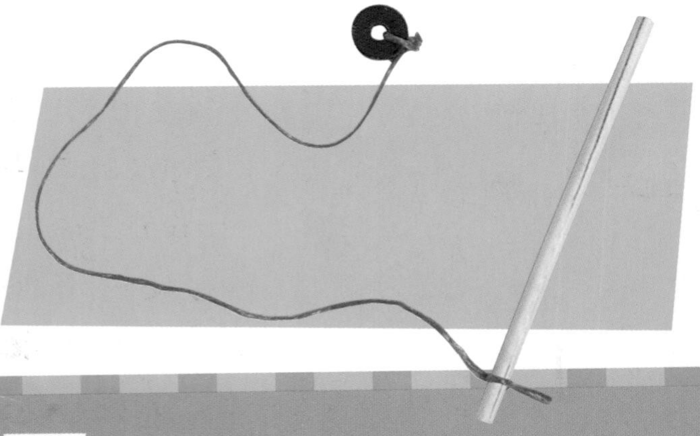

2 Cut some fish shapes out of the card. Number each fish. Attach a paperclip to each fish.

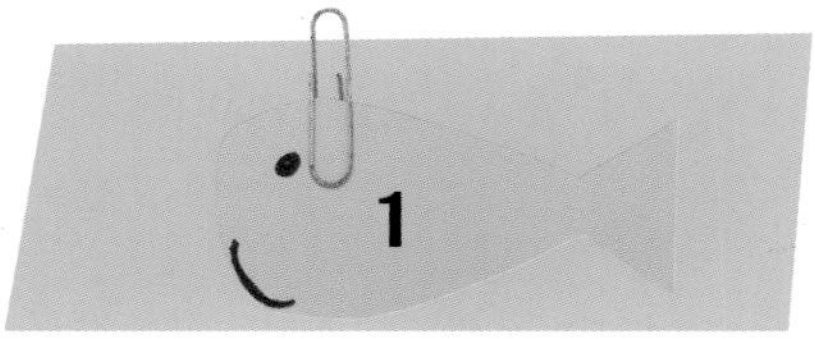

3 Put the fish on the ground or in a large bowl.

4 Lower the magnet over the fish. Can you catch any fish? If you play with a friend you can take it in turns to fish. When all the fish have been caught, add up the numbers on your 'catch' and see who has the highest score.

Because . . .

The magnet pulls the fish off the ground because the paperclip on the fish sticks to the magnet. This is because the magnet is pulling the metal paperclip towards it. Most magnets are made of the metals iron or ***steel****. There is also a magnetic rock called* ***lodestone*** *(left) or magnetite.*

Magnetic materials

Some objects stick to magnets and others do not.

THINK about where you would find magnets in your home.

- Fridge doors have small magnets in them to hold the door shut.
- Fridge magnets can decorate the fridge door.

What sort of objects stick to magnets?

You will need:

A pencil and a ruler ✓

A sheet of paper ✓

A strong magnet, such as a bar magnet ✓

Some test objects (e.g. a coin, an eraser, a key, a wooden spoon, a metal spoon, a plastic cup, some drawing pins, some scraps of paper) ✓

Which materials are magnetic?

1. Use the pencil and ruler to divide your paper into three columns. Name the first column 'object', the second column 'guess', and the third column 'result'.

2 Write a list of your test objects in the first column.

3 In the second column, put a tick next to the objects you think will stick to the magnet, and a cross next to those you think will not.

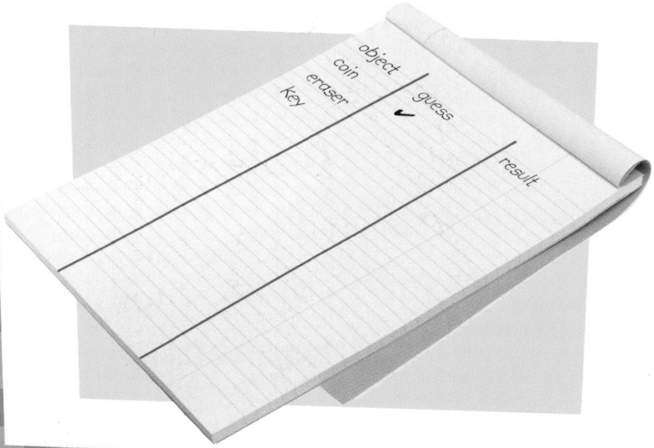

4 Test each object in turn and put a tick or a cross in the third column. How many of your guesses were correct?

Because . . .

Objects stick to magnets because they have iron in them. Materials that have iron in them are called ***magnetic materials****. Materials with no iron in them, such as tin, brass, paper and wood, are non-magnetic and do not stick to magnets.*

⚠ Do not test your magnets on music or video tapes and discs. Do not use magnets near televisions and computers – the magnets could damage them.

Pulling power

A **force** is a pull or push. The pulling power of magnets is a force called **magnetism**.

THINK about different kinds of force.

- You lift a glass using the force of your muscles.
- A magnet pulls on a paperclip using magnetism.

Can you see magnetism work?

You will need:

A pen and a ruler ✔

A piece of paper ✔

A strong bar magnet ✔

Some paperclips ✔

A horseshoe magnet ✔

How does magnetism work?

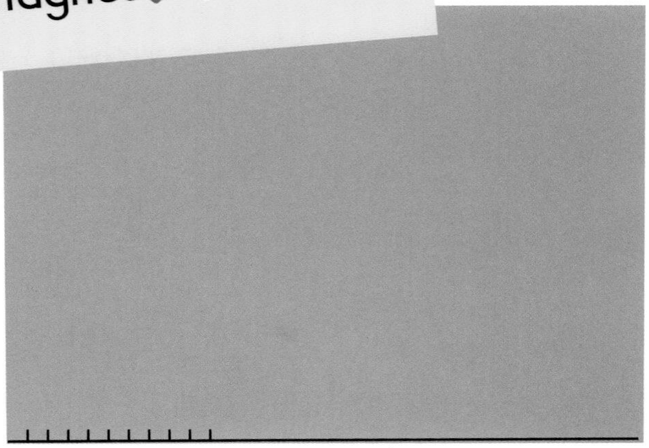

1. Use the ruler to draw a straight line along the long edge of the paper. Mark each centimetre for 10 cm from the top of the piece of paper, as shown.

2 Draw a line across the page at the 10 cm and 1 cm marks. These are your start and finish lines.

3 Place the bar magnet on the start line and the paperclip on the finish line.

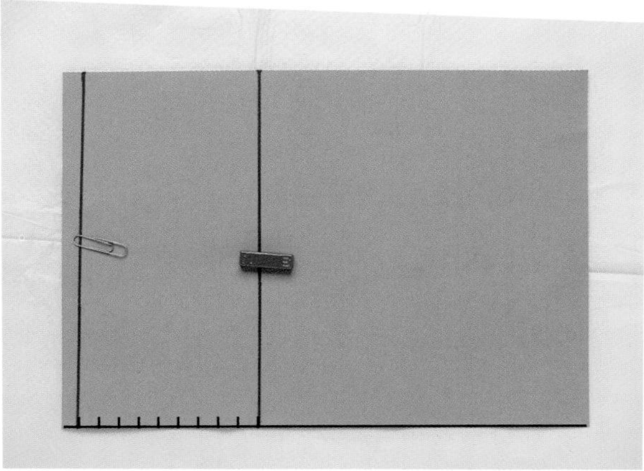

4 Slowly slide the bar magnet along the paper towards the paperclip. How far away is the magnet from the paperclip before anything happens?

5 Try the test again using the horseshoe magnet instead of the bar magnet. What happens?

Because . . .

*The paperclip moves towards the magnet because it is **attracted**, or pulled, to the magnet by the force of magnetism. Magnets have different strengths. How far away the magnet is before it attracts the paperclip depends on the strength of your magnet.*

Poles apart

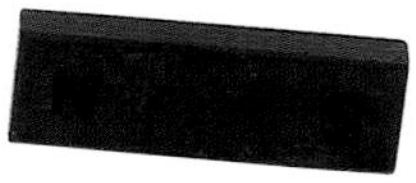

Magnetism is stronger at the ends of a magnet than in the middle.

THINK about a bar magnet.

- The ends of a magnet are known as its **poles**.
- Sometimes the poles are different colours. They may also be marked with the letters 'N' and 'S', for north and south pole.

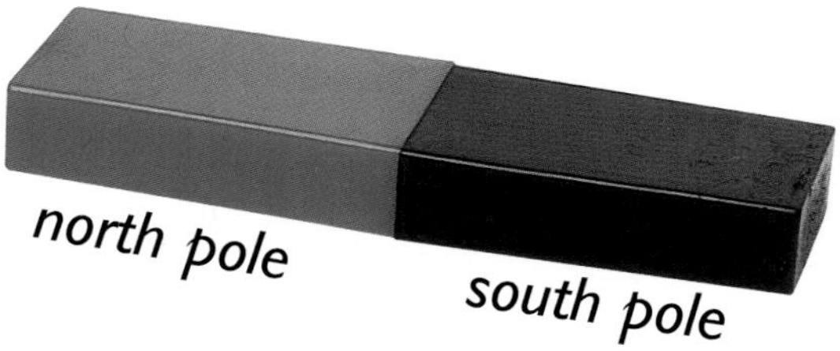

How are the poles of a magnet different?

You will need:

Some tape ✓

2 toy cars ✓

2 bar magnets at least as long as the cars ✓

What happens when different poles touch?

1. Tape the middle of each magnet to the roof of a toy car. Make sure both magnets have the same pole pointing to the front of the car.

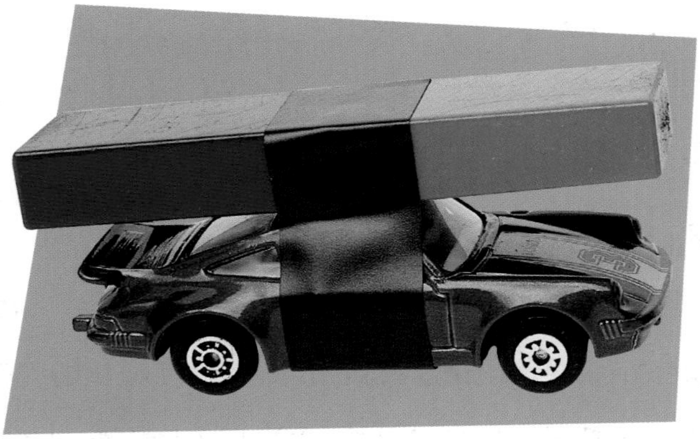

2. What happens when you push the front of one car towards the back of the other?

3. What happens when you push both cars face to face?

4. What happens if you put the cars back to back?

Because . . .

When one car is behind the other, the magnets pull the cars together. This is because the opposite poles are facing each other (north to south, or south to north). Opposite magnetic poles attract each other.

When the two cars are facing each other or when they are back to back, the magnets push the cars apart. This is because the same poles are facing each other (north to north or south to south). The same magnetic poles ***repel****, or push away from, each other.*

An invisible force

Magnetism is an invisible force – you cannot see it. It can pull on things without touching them.

THINK about how magnetism works.

- The paperclip on pages 10–11 jumped towards the magnet before the magnet touched it.
- Magnetism can reach through the air to pull on something.

How far does magnetism reach?

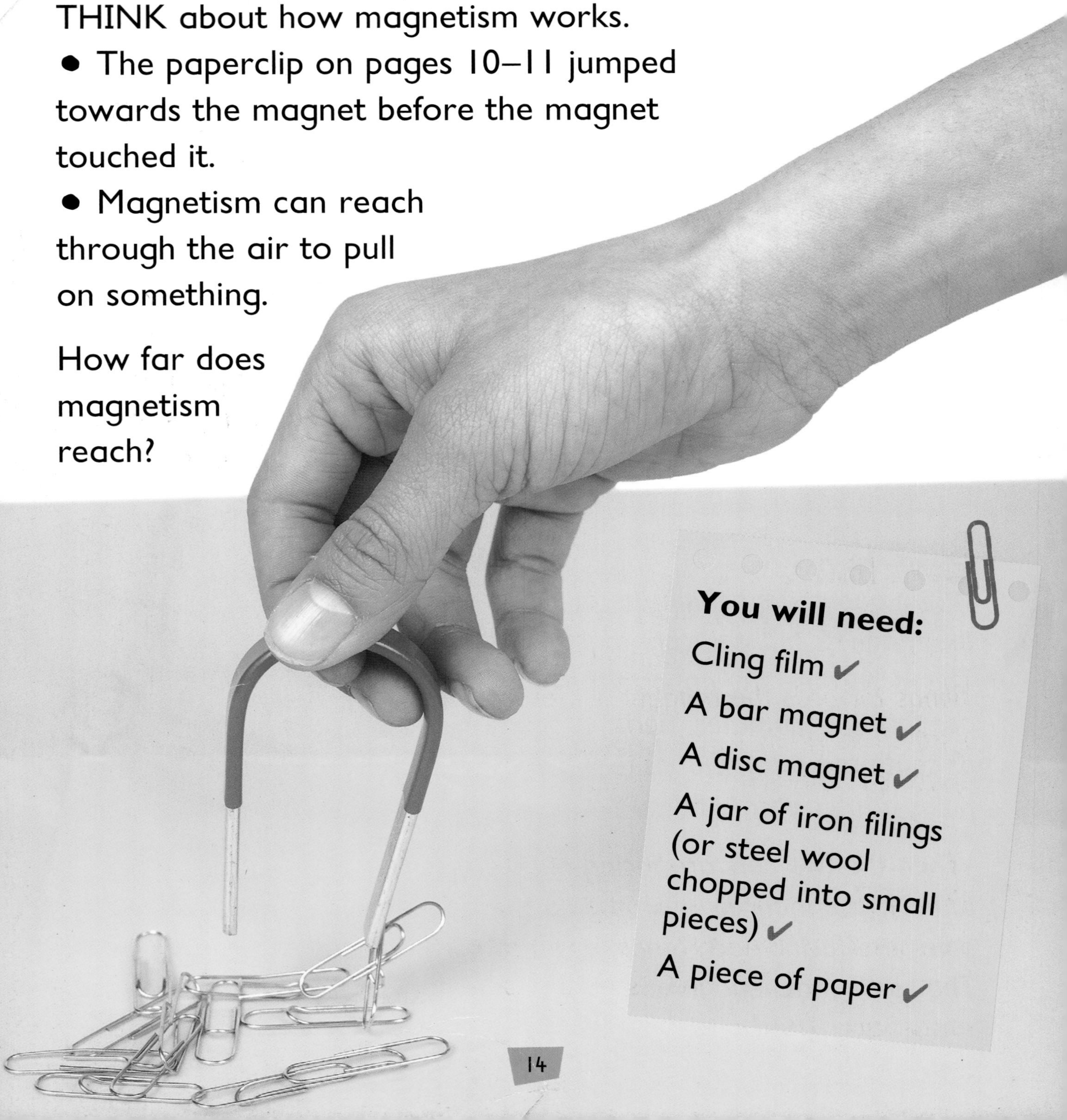

You will need:

Cling film ✓

A bar magnet ✓

A disc magnet ✓

A jar of iron filings (or steel wool chopped into small pieces) ✓

A piece of paper ✓

How does magnetism surround a magnet?

1. Wrap both magnets in cling film. Place the paper on top of the bar magnet, so that the magnet is in the middle.

2. Sprinkle the iron filings (or steel wool) onto the paper, around the spot where the magnet is. What happens?

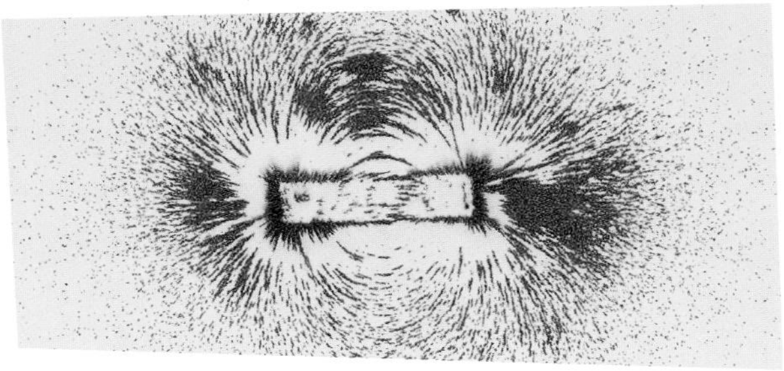

3. Lift the paper up and carefully pour your filings back into the jar.

4. Replace the bar magnet with the disc magnet. Shake the filings onto the paper again. What happens this time?

Because . . .

The iron filings form lines on the paper showing how the magnetic force (magnetism) pulls the iron filings towards the magnet. Different-shaped magnets make different patterns. The filings are usually thickest at the poles, but other lines spread out from the magnet, or curve from pole to pole. These lines show how far from the magnet its magnetic force reaches. This area is called its ***magnetic field****.*

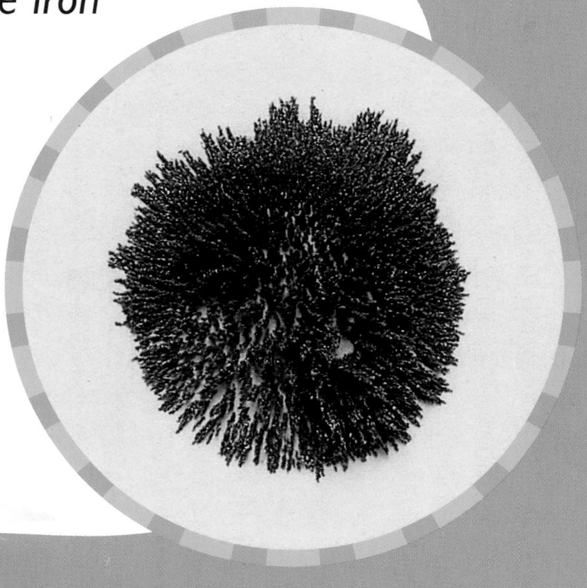

Strength of force

A magnetic field can reach through non-magnetic materials.

THINK about what fridge magnets do.

- A fridge magnet will hold a piece of paper on to a magnetic surface, such as a metal door.
- But paper is non-magnetic and will not stick to the magnet on its own.

How strong is a magnetic field?

You will need:

- Scissors ✔
- Paper ✔
- A bar magnet ✔
- Sticky tape ✔
- A paperclip ✔

How strong is a magnetic field?

1 Cut the paper into several squares. Make the squares large enough to wrap around the magnet.

2 Check that the magnet will pick up the paperclip.

3 Wrap the magnet in one layer of paper and pick up the paperclip.

4 Repeat step 3 a number of times, adding an extra layer of paper each time.

5 How do the different layers of paper affect the magnet?

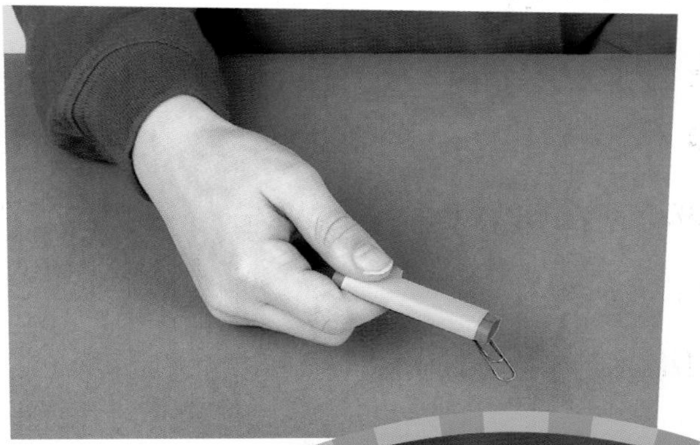

Because . . .

The magnet should pick up the paperclip through at least one layer of paper. This is because its magnetic force spreads outwards, as we saw on pages 14–15. But if the magnet is wrapped in layer upon layer of paper, the layers will gradually block the magnetic force and the magnet will no longer work.

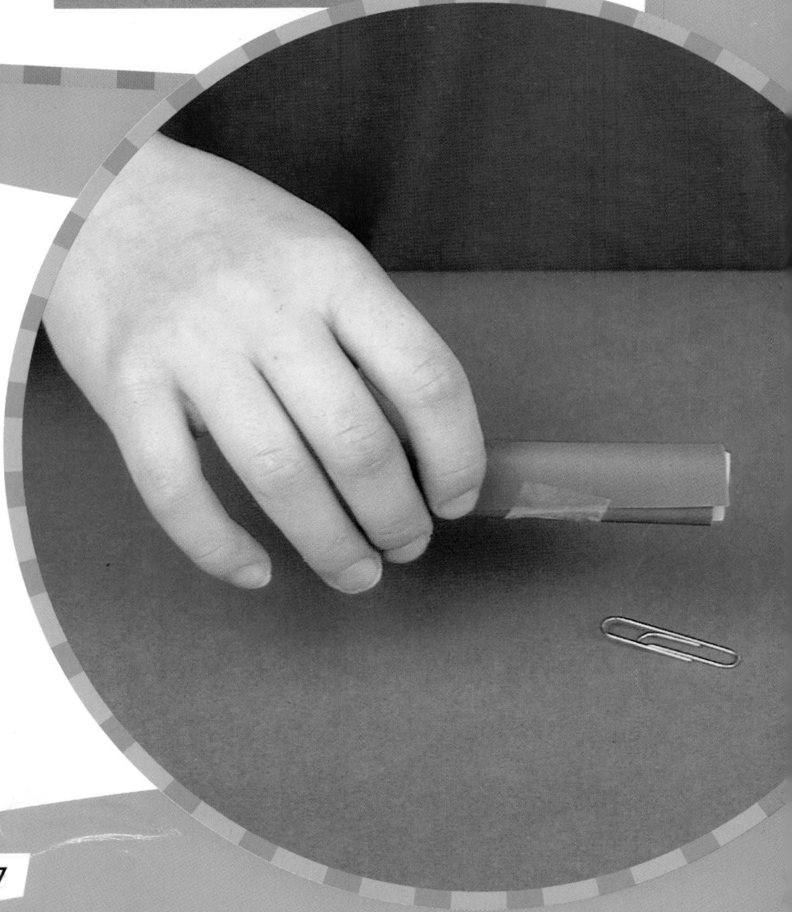

Magnetic magic

Magnetism can work through most materials, including water.

THINK about what water is.
- Everything in the world is made of some kind of material.
- Water is a liquid material. It flows in streams, lakes, seas and oceans.

Can you use a magnet to pull something out of water?

You will need:
A glass jar ✔
Water ✔
A paperclip ✔
A magnet ✔
Some string ✔

Do magnets work through water?

1. Almost fill the glass jar with water.

2 Drop in the paperclip and let it sink to the bottom of the jar.

3 What happens if you hold the magnet to the outside of the jar near the paperclip? Can you make the paperclip move? Can you lift it to the top of the jar?

4 Repeat step 2, but this time tie a length of string around the magnet and lower it into the water. Will it pick up the paperclip?

Because . . .

You can use the magnet to slide the paperclip up the side of the glass jar because its magnetic field passes through the glass and the water to pull on the paperclip. If you put the magnet into the water it will still work on the paperclip – because water is non-magnetic and does not block the magnetic field.

Moving with magnets

The pulling power of magnets can be used in different ways.

You will need:

- A permanent marker ✔
- A large piece of stiff card ✔
- 2 pieces of thin card about 5 cm square ✔
- 4 food cans ✔
- 2 paperclips ✔
- 2 disc magnets ✔
- 2 rulers ✔
- Sticky tape ✔
- Scissors ✔
- A watch ✔

THINK about how magnets are used to move things.

- A crane with a large magnet hanging from it is used to lift and move heavy blocks of metal in a scrap-yard.

How can you use magnets?

Can you make a magnetic game?

1. Use the permanent marker to draw a wiggly road on the large piece of card.

2 Make a fold across the middle of each thin card. Draw the shape of a car on the card above the fold. Cut the fold into two flaps and fold them in opposite directions so that the cars stand upright.

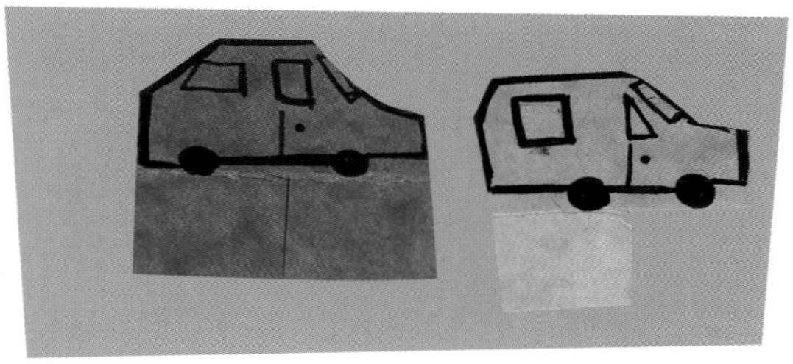

3 Prop up the large card with cans at each corner so there is a clear gap beneath it. Slide a paperclip onto the front flap of each car and place the cars at the start of the road.

4 Tape a magnet to the end of each ruler and slide the magnets underneath the large card to move the cars. How long does it take each player to move their car to the end of the road?

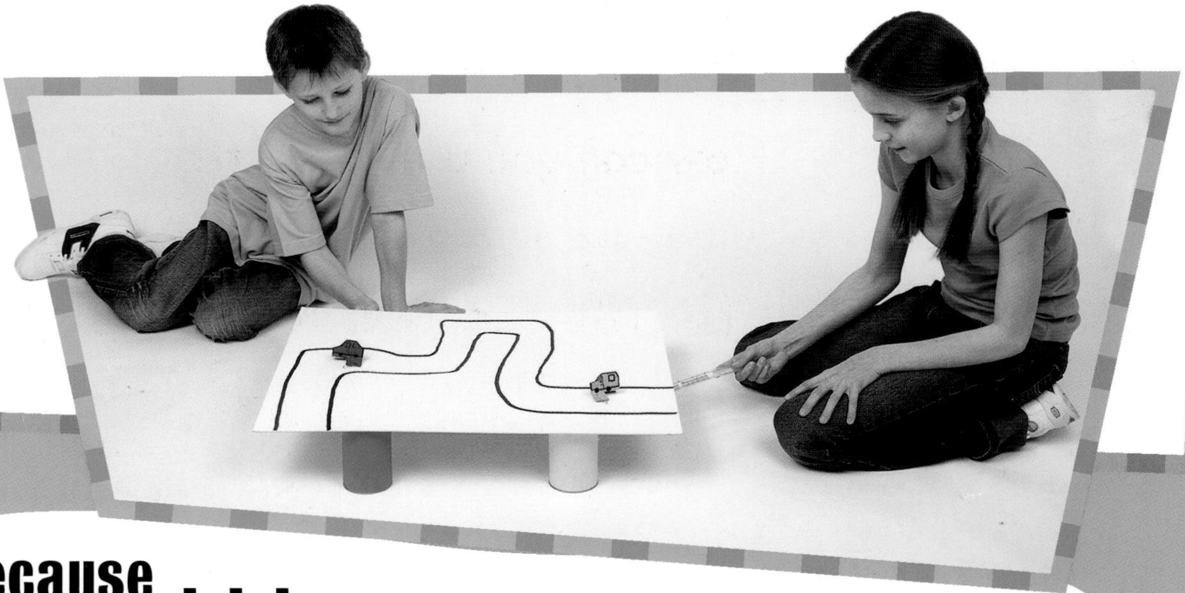

Because . . .

The magnets are able to move the cars around the road because their magnetic force passes through the card and attracts the metal paperclips attached to the cars.

Sorting with magnets

Magnets can be used to separate some materials from others.

THINK about how magnets are used to separate things.

- Magnets separate iron and steel from other materials in a scrap-yard.
- Iron and steel are often recycled (used again). Magnets separate steel cans from aluminium cans so they can be recycled.

Why not make your own can sorter?

You will need:
Some string ✔
A strong magnet ✔
Some clean, empty food and drink cans ✔

What kind of metal is it?

1. Tie a length of string as long as your leg to the magnet.

2. Stand the cans in a line on the floor.

3. Hold the string in your hand and let the magnet dangle over the cans. Slowly move it along the line of cans. What happens? Which cans are attracted to the magnet, and which ones are not?

Because . . .

Some of the cans will be attracted to the magnet, but others will not. This is because some cans are made of steel, which is a magnetic material, and some are made of aluminium, which is a non-magnetic material. Which types of food and drink are stored in steel cans and which types are stored in aluminium cans?

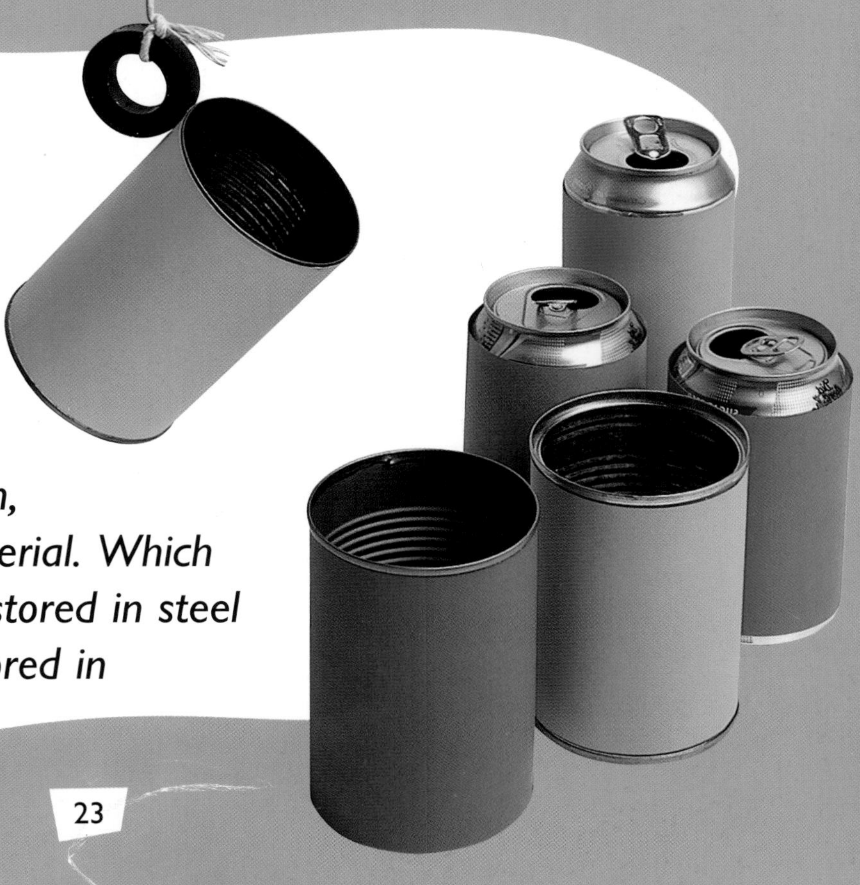

Floating with magnets

The pushing force of magnets is also useful.

THINK about how magnets repel (push away from) each other.

- The cars on pages 12–13 repelled each other when they were facing back to back.

Can you use this pushing force to make a magnet float?

You will need:

3 doughnut magnets ✔

Coloured paper ✔

Scissors ✔

A glue stick or sticky tape ✔

A piece of dowelling rod almost as thick as the hole in the magnets ✔

Plasticine ✔

How can you make magnets float?

1. Find out which side of your magnets stick together. As opposite poles attract, one side will be a north pole, the other a south pole.

2. Cut out and glue or tape a small square of coloured paper onto the north side of each magnet.

3. Push the dowelling rod into a lump of Plasticine so that it stands upright.

4. Slide magnet 1 onto the dowelling rod north side up, magnet 2 north side down, and magnet 3 north side up. What happens to the magnets?

Because . . .

The magnets float apart because they all have the same poles facing each other. North to north or south to south poles repel each other. Without the dowelling rod the magnets would slip sideways and drop to the table, but the rod holds them in place, keeping the poles facing each other.

Index